The Hindu Epics – An Introduction to Ancient India's Defining Masterpieces.

KIRAN ATMA

Copyright © 2023 Kiran Atma

All rights reserved. No part of this publication may be reproduced, stored in a retrieval system, or transmitted in any form or by any means or including electronic, mechanical, photocopying, recording, or otherwise without prior written permission from the publisher.

This publication is intended for informational purposes only. Any trademarks are the property of their respective owners, are used for editorial purposes only, and the publisher makes no claim of ownership and shall acquire no right, title or interest in such trademarks by virtue of this publication.

ISBN: 9798390038130

DEDICATION

This book is dedicated to Religious Liberty and Freedom of Faith, a notion that protects an individual's or a community's right to demonstrate religion or belief through instruction, practice, worship, and observance, whether in public or private.

The Indian Epics provide a wealth of knowledge about India's science, traditions, religion, and arts at different points throughout its history. They serve as an enormous collection of human knowledge.

CONTENTS

1	Introduction	7
2	Ramayana – Rama's Sojourn	20
3	The Slaying of Ravana	41
4	Mahabharata - The Bharata Dynasty's Great Saga	68
5	Battles of the Great War	87
6	Lessons of the Epics	109

1 INTRODUCTION

The Epics grow from the ashes of the Vedic writings, which place a strong emphasis on fire sacrifices. The link goes beyond being lyrical. The more militaristic age of the Epics preached a "sacrifice of battle"—war—as the ideal method of approaching the Absolute, much like Vedic religion, which was centered on the sacrificial arena, with intricate fire rites and Brahmin priests who were particularly educated to conduct them.

The objective remained the same: to uphold dharma, or cosmic order, by making an all-consuming sacrifice for the sake of the spirit. The Epic battles were recreations of the conflicts between good and evil depicted in Vedic scriptures, in which gods engaged in combat with demons and light was set against darkness. These gods and demons were not ordinary ones. The same characters from the Vedic texts, such as the Pandava princes, who were all semidivine creatures, resurface in fresh incarnations with exactly the same characteristics.

But the Epics transport us to a period when chivalry appeared more significant than fire offerings and Brahminical rites were overshadowed by kingly ones. Not that the Epics are devoid of Brahminical culture; rather, it is rather that this culture is subordinated to the Kshatriyas, the military class of ancient India.

All of this, of course, serves to make the Vedic fundamental principles more understandable and accessible to the general public. Vyasa, who compiled the Vedas and wrote the Mahabharata, purposefully based his later work on a military theme. He did so because they lived in the Kali-yuga, our present period of strife and hypocrisy. People connect to conflict since it is prevalent in this time period. The Mahabharata combat account, still fresh in people's minds, was thus ideal for Vyasa's purposes—he would write a book based on recent historical events that was suited for the period.

A good narrative has love, hate, jealousy, intrigue, chivalry, moral education, and plenty of action. The events in this novel included all of those things. Hence, he was able to communicate the Vedic principles to his Kali-yuga audience inside the framework of an engaging story. While it described events that took place far earlier and was written by the renowned poet Valmiki rather than Vyasa, the Ramayana performed a similar function.

The Mahabharata and the Ramayana, two of India's greatest epics and foundational texts for modern Hinduism, both center on the supreme deity Vishnu and his two most adored incarnations, Krishna and Rama. As the Vedic scriptures do not have such a clearly defined deity, some academics contend that the theistic aspect of Hinduism is a relatively recent development that began with the Epics.

Nevertheless, according to legend, these same fundamental truths were concealed in the ancient Vedic language and could only be discovered by studying the scriptures with a genuine guru. These Epic books include a richness of philosophy and religion, as well as instructions for living a moral and upright life, all of which are woven throughout the tales that make up its heart.

The Mahabharata and the Ramayana have therefore proved to be of great value to numerous individuals over the ages. Yet millions of people throughout the globe still find value in them. Moreover, knowledge of these Epics is crucial for comprehending the Hindu way of thinking.

These two enormous texts provide the majority of the philosophical and cultural foundations for contemporary Hinduism. Hence, for those who may not have read them cover to cover, this chapter will summarize, explain, and contextualize them. It should be noted that as they are among of the longest works in literature, we will have to omit certain details and shorten others in our recounting. This work, which is found in the Ramayana, the oldest of the two, has the distinction of being referred to as the earliest poetry in the canon of Sanskrit literature.

According to legend, Rama lived during the Treta-yuga era, which is said to have existed millions of years before the Treta-yuga of more recent memory. In terms of length, the Ramayana surpasses well-known Western epics like the Iliad and the Odyssey, which contain just 15,693 lines and 12,000 lines, respectively. It is made up of around 24,000 couplets (48,000 lines). Of fact, there are considerably over 100,000 lines in the Mahabharata.

The Ramayana, which is the oldest of these manuscripts, has been likened to the well-known Greek Epics in terms of style, and since these works contain certain same themes, the Ramayana is frequently considered to be the source upon which the Odyssey, in particular, was founded. Rama, for instance, does what Menelaus did when he destroyed Troy and brought Helen back: he vanquishes the ten-headed evil Ravana and saves his beloved bride Sita.

Both Greek tragedy and the Sanskrit Epic's commentarial tradition attempt to address issues in a similar manner. For instance, the poet Stesichorus claimed that Helen never actually traveled to Troy with Paris; rather, the Helen in Troy was a substitute apparition, and the real Helen patiently awaited her beloved Menelaus in Egypt, just as the pure-hearted Sita, according to tradition, could not have been captured, or even touched, by a demon such as Ravana.

Similar to this, the Rama legends describe another Sita—a "shadow" or "illusory" Sita—who was taken by Ravana as the "genuine" Sita waited for Rama in an unmanifest form. Due to these connections, academics are presently examining how the ancient Indian

epics influenced Western civilization. The
Ramayana is valuable as ancient literature, but
its best quality is its pure beauty—beauty in
the form of its profound Sanskrit poetry and
the thought-provoking commentary that
comes from each main character's lips.

It is beautiful in terms of its exotic settings in
the forest and its magnificent cities, which are
depicted in graphic detail. It is beautiful in
terms of its deeply philosophical dialogue and
the morals and ethics it instills in its readers. It
is beautiful in terms of its sense of dharma
and the importance of doing one's duty. It is
beautiful in terms of the emotions it evokes.

But, perhaps most importantly, it is beautiful
in terms of the characters one meets during a
thorough journey through its pages. Of
course, Rama is the foremost among them.
He is the epitome of virtue—tall, powerful,
and righteous—and a real hero who isn't
ashamed to display his more human side, to
love, or to experience separation agony when
the person he holds dear is taken from him.
He is the divine in the flesh. The lady in issue,

Sita, is not devoid of virtues; in fact, she is the exact embodiment of chastity and everything that is right and noble. She is the most significant character in the whole narrative and is clever, independent, and strong-willed.

Then there are Rama's younger brothers, Lakshman being the most notable. Lakshman, who never leaves Rama's side, is dearer to Rama than life itself since he has all of Rama's admirable traits, much like his other two brothers, Bharata and Shatrughna.

Hanuman is also one of the most well-known characters from the Ramayana, and because of his intense devotion to Rama, bhakti cults have developed around him as their main idol. Yet, to idolize someone or anything but Rama would be to misunderstand the essence of the Ramayana. Hanuman himself repeats Rama's name—a term meaning "the utmost pleasure," invoking thoughts of the Absolute Being and how the most profound satisfaction comes from worshiping Him.

In fact, even Hanuman would avoid people

who worship him (Hanuman), stating, "I, too, am only a devotee of Ramachandra." Once again, the original narrator of Rama's tale was a woodland dweller called Valmiki who, before becoming a sage-poet, was an infamous felon.

He was once invited to recite the Lord's name by the renowned saint Narada, who had arrived upon his hermitage. Valmiki, though, retorted that he would not. Narada, however, was crafty, and he asked Valmiki if he would instead focus on himself as a murderer, saying, "I am a murderer and a thief, and I have nothing to do with the devout activities of religious practitioners." Valmiki decided to do this, and instantly went on to adopt mara as his own personal mantra. Narada informed him he could achieve this by only repeating the word mara, which means "death."

By rapidly repeating "mara, mara, mara," he discovered that the word got inverted, and that he was really saying "Rama, Rama, Rama." As a result, his heart was cleaned by the power of pronouncing the name of God.

He created the Ramayana as a consequence, which is the most thorough account of Rama legend in the vast body of Vaishnava literature.

Even though it is elaborate, the story of Rama has been repeated and interpreted in a variety of ways, as can be seen in the many regional variations in local dialects. The substance of the tale may be summed up as follows for our needs.

The Ultimate Lord visited Earth in the form of Ramachandra, a human prince, millions of years ago.

Why did God become a human being? The narrative starts when a group of demigods go to their lord, Lord Brahma, and express worry about a demon-king named Ravana who is pillaging the Earth. Ravana had grown almost invincible as a result of the demon's severe penances, and Brahma had granted him a blessing (and Brahma's boons always come true) stating that he "could never be beaten in combat, neither by god nor by any celestial creature." Yet, as humans were not specifically mentioned in Brahma's blessing, it was still conceivable for a highly skilled human, someone who was more powerful than any angel or demigod (if such a creature existed), to perhaps defeat him. Ravana naturally reasoned that this was impossible and that his boon had made him invincible since a simple human could never beat a greater creature.

But the worried gods started to think about how they might utilize this gap in Brahma's favor to terminate Ravana's reign of terror. Just then, Lord Vishnu appeared and gave them the assurance that He would take the form of a human called Ramachandra and thereby slay the demon, Ravana.

Rama defeated the demon king thanks to his human incarnation, and he also set a great example for how people should behave. He demonstrates that the real hero is not some idealized representation of perfection but rather a loving, feeling, morally upright person who nevertheless has "imperfections," which makes him fully entire. According to

Ramayana expert Ranchor Prime, Rama is God manifest and the seventh manifestation of Vishnu. He made the decision to forget who he really was—divine—for the length of his human existence and instead choose to become human.

He experienced emotional and bodily suffering after losing his beloved Sita. Rama's voyage might be seen as an analogy for the journey that every soul must take. In taking on human form, Rama joined in our pain and played out the drama of our own lives.

Each of us experiences exile, grief, and disillusionment on our own terms, and finally aspires to come to terms with our lot and achieve ultimate redemption. As a result, hearing or seeing Rama suffer is like reliving our own existence, but in a supernatural setting.

Every chapter of the epic has several layers that explore both the divine lila of Rama and each character's own karma, or fate. Similar to this, modern-day Vedic sages in India assert that life itself is the process by which each of us works out our unique web of karma, desires, and free will in harmony or opposition with God's plan.

Rama's divinity is always on Valmiki's mind, even though he often presents Rama as the ideal person, complete with parents, friends, and other relationships. Early on, he refers to Rama's heavenly birth (1.17.6) and repeatedly demonstrates his devotion to Vishnu. Nevertheless, the tale is more nuanced than that.

2 RAMAYANA – RAMA'S SOJOURN

According to Valmiki, when Lord Rama manifests as a human being on earth, he does so as the son of King Dasharath and Queen Kaushalya, descended from Ikshvaku, the first king of the world. He comes from the most fortunate line of the ruling elite and is born during the Sun dynasty. His parents adore him as a little kid, and Ayodhya, the former capital of a single global monarchy, adores him as well. Sumitra and Kaikeyi are the other two principal Queens of Dasharath, and as we'll see, they also have important roles to play in Rama's tale. According to Valmiki, Rama has all the excellent traits of a great leader and has had them since he was a little child. He is exceptionally physically strong, beautiful, wise, famous, and wealthy, but he is also unusually modest and renounced.

In fact, he is so renounced that he can easily leave up his beloved kingdom and live a simple life in the forest—a tale we shall return to shortly. His younger brother Lakshman is inseparable from him. Lakshman, albeit of a different mother, Sumitra, one of King Dasharath's three primary wives, is like a mirror of Rama, equal to him in the aforementioned virtues. Rama's physical appearance is that of young, green grass, and his demeanor is grounded and unforced, much like the forest where he spends the most of his time on earth.

Lakshman, on the other hand, has a golden color. They thus seem to be men, but their distinctive coloring and superhuman abilities serve as frequent reminders that they are not like other men. Like Rama himself, Lakshman is a powerful fighter. Together, the two brothers arrive on Earth to defeat the army of man-eating Rakshasa warriors led by the seemingly unbeatable warlord King Ravana.

Rama's adventures are really first mentioned when he is only 16 years old. He hasn't had official training yet, but his reputation as a great archer already precedes him.

Vishvamitra, a then-famous yogi, visits King Dasharath and requests that his highly capable son accompany him on a crucial military mission: A group of formidable Rakshasas are assaulting the hermitages of holy people and interfering with the conduct of religious rituals. As he is still a young man and a green as a warrior (excuse the pun), the only one who can make things right, only the pure and strong Rama would be able to assist. This Vishvamitra is confident of it. Dasharath hesitates by nature. He doesn't want his child to take part in a mission that may be fatal.

Dasharath, who also believes that only Rama can bring the formidable Rakshasas to their knees, decides to let Rama escape when Vishvamitra expresses the gravity of the situation. The godly youngster bravely pursues Vishvamitra into the forest with nothing more than a bow and arrow (albeit it is far from an ordinary bow and arrow).

Lakshman, who is constantly at his side, is with him. The celestial brothers desire solely to fight on the side of justice because they trust the sages to be nice people. While in the jungle, Vishvamitra teaches the lads, who are already skilled, how to cast heavenly spells and use amazing weapons. They are excellent trainees.

Rama's bow was a gift from the deity Indra, and when combined with his collection of lethal arrows and the might of mantra (mystic incantations with supernatural power), he had the strength of a thousand warriors. As committed to his goal as Hanuman will be when they eventually cross paths, his arrows won't stray from their target once they've been discharged. Rama is the ultimate heavenly archer.

Jumping forward can help you understand

this: in the ultimate conflict with Ravana, Rama employs the Brahmashtra, a nuclear-powered arrow whose intense heat is claimed to terrify the inhabitants of the farthest planets in the material world.

According to Vaishnava literature, God is by definition the greatest in all domains, as Lord Krishna declares in the Bhagavad-Gita, "Among sword wielders, I am Rama." A careful study of the Ramayana reveals that he is also the best fighter.

To go back to our narrative, Rama and Vishvamitra had a successful excursion. But, when the first of these Rakshasas is brought before him, Rama declines to take any action since the demon is a lady and his chivalrous nature forbids him from killing a person of the fairer sex.

As Lakshman notices Rama's hesitation and the demon's unrelenting destruction of woodland hermitages, he bravely shoots the demon with a single arrow. The dynamic brothers then vanquish other woodland monsters, including Maricha. Rama fires a "wind arrow" at this specific demon, which launches him thousands of miles into the air before splashing him into the water.

While he is not killed by this deed, he is sufficiently degraded and flees. Later on, he would show up as one of Rama's significant adversaries. Vishvamitra, who is delighted with young Rama, assumes the role of his guru and tells him a variety of magnificent Vedic tales while emphasizing on the important teachings they provide.

Also, he shares with Rama information on a superb bow owned by Sita's father, King Janaka.

According to legend, Janaka once helped Lord Shiva, and as a reward, he was given Shiva's enchanted bow, which is regarded among demigods as the best weapon. The bow seems like a fitting gift since Janaka is a warrior-king. But it is so big and strong that no one could even bend it to connect the string to it. Janaka reasoned that the bow could only be used by someone who is powerful and moral, like the demigod who gave it to him as a reward. As a result, he considered it to be a holy item deserving of respect. He often knelt before it, prayed, and sent flowers in hopes of one day seeing a supernatural being who could thread it and harness its incredible power.

In fact, King Janaka made his daughter Sita available for marriage to any man who knew how to handle a bow correctly. Of course, Sita was coveted by many. Her dowry was unparalleled bravery and the goodwill of God Himself; nonetheless, even the most noble and strong of men were unable to gain her hand. Janaka cherished her as his most precious love object since she was the crown gem of his empire.

Vishvamitra invites Rama and Lakshman to Janaka's palace after learning about Shiva's bow, solely to show them this marvelous creation of the gods. A sizable crowd has gathered to see the weapon as the three guys enter. Rama picks it up right away, which is a marvel in and of itself, and asks Janaka, "What should I do with it? Do you want it strung for you? "Sure," Janaka responds incredulously. Rama quickly threads the bow and bends it in front of everyone.

He ties the string on the bow so firmly that it splits in two, creating a tremendous boom that knocks everyone out save for Vishvamitra, Rama, and Lakshman asleep. The skies are filled with joy as Lord Rama is showered with flowers from the gods at that very time.

Rama's ability to string Shiva's bow has mythological significance, much like Thor, who is the only living creature capable of using his hammer, or Arthur, who is the only person capable of removing his magical sword from its stone.

Another similarity may be drawn with King Odysseus in Homer's Odyssey, who raises a magical bow to display his bravery and power upon his return from the Trojan War.

Soon, truth and happiness will be accessible to everyone thanks to the love of Sita and

Rama—the Ultimate Love—which will blossom on Earth. King Janaka declares that his daughter should be married to the powerful Ramachandra as soon as the gathered participants awaken from their sleep and return to their senses.

Now, Sita approaches Rama and presents him with fresh flowers as a sign of her acceptance of him as her husband. Lakshman marries Urmila, Sita's sister, while Rama's other two brothers, Bharata and Shutrughna, marry her two cousins on the same day they are married.

Hindu legend holds that Sita is not a typical human. It is understood that Sita is truly Lakshmi, the Goddess of Fortune, the Lord's feminine counterpart in the spiritual realm, just as Lord Rama is Vishnu, the Almighty Lord Himself. She goes by the name Janaki and incarnates as Janaka's daughter. King Janaka wasn't Sita's real father; he just happened to find her when she was a newborn. She was hiding in a pile of dirt when King Janaka, who was plowing a field, saw her.

According to the Ramayana, Sita was truly created right from the Earth with the intention of ending Ravana's rule since the demon was contaminating the globe with his actions. It seemed as if the Earth was retaliating by purging itself of its most opulent contaminants.

When Rama takes on the roles of the greatest warrior, preacher of morals, and exponent of religion, Sita assumes the role of the greatest female beauty, weakening Ravana with her inherent allure. Rama, Sita, Lakshman, and their other brothers all live happily in Ayodhya for a period of time.

As he approaches old age, King Dasharath chooses to give the throne to his beloved oldest son Rama. The inhabitants of Ayodhya begin to joyfully prepare for the ritual as word of Rama's impending coronation spreads. Nevertheless, destiny has other plans: Manthara, an orphan girl who now serves as Queen Kaikeyi's maidservant, was reared by Queen Kaikeyi, Dasharath's bride and the mother of the noble Bharata. The malicious seed that sprouts into the tree of disaster in the Ramayana was sown by Manthara. When she learns that Rama has been crowned king, she is enraged beyond measure. She rushes into Queen Kaikeyi's chamber full of resentment and claims that Rama's coronation is the worst thing that could have happened—a smack in the face to the monarch. Manthara deftly describes how Dasharath just sent Bharata to see his uncle.

She claims that he carried out this action so that Rama may be crowned King without any interference. Rama would undoubtedly see to it that Bharata was assassinated after the coronation because he would never allow his younger brother to usurp the kingdom. Manthara instills jealousy and fury in the Queen's heart by foreseeing all the suffering that lies ahead for Kaikeyi with such twisted reasoning.

For the benefit of her own son, Queen Kaikeyi is now persuaded that Rama must be destroyed. She is obviously precious to him since she is Dasharath's wife and because of a promise he made to her in the past, she will be able to accomplish her goals. It seems that Dasharath had previously been severely injured in a battlefield.

Queen Kaikeyi had then tenderly nurtured him back to health. Upon seeing her adoration, he made her two promises: everything she want. But she had already said that she would request them later. It was now time, inspired by Manthara.

In her private room, Kaikeyi is waiting for Dasharath to arrive. Her presence causes the coronation day to be infected like a snake biting an innocent kid as he arrives and discovers her there.

She then requests the following two boons in accordance with your promise: first, let Ramachandra be exiled to the jungle for 14 years; and, second, let my son Bharata be enthroned as king in his place.

Unable to endure the ramifications of her words, Dasharath passes out. Oh, how sad! he cries as he awakens. Such a hassle! Even if I find it quite painful to hear what you have to say, I am obligated by an oath to do so. I must be suffering right now because of sins from a former life!

Why Dasharath does not just turn down the Queen's request is a mystery. He is unable to, is the response. In the era of the Ramayana, warrior-kings kept their promise as if their own existence relied on it.

Being a Kshatriya (a noble administrator), he was obligated to keep the commitment he had made. Integrity was his faith. He must now fulfill Kaikeyi's requests, whatever they may be, for he promised to give her any two boons when she saved his life.

On the same day of Rama's coronation, Dasharath calls him to his palace. Rama looks to be radiating with brilliance as he pulls up in his chariot to answer his father's summons, just as the moon comes out from behind a bank of dark blue clouds. When he stands by his side, Lakshman uses a unique fan to cool him. His chariot is followed by elephants and horses, and the scene is filled with music, glory, and applause. Beautiful ladies and regal monarchs toss vibrant flowers from their windows as he goes by, which fall down all around him.

Some bystanders laud Sita as a pearl among women and claim that she must have performed significant penances in previous lifetimes to have such a spouse as this king-to-be. Others praise Kaushalya, the mother of Rama. The ancient King, who is reclining on a couch with Queen Kaikeyi, seems distraught when Rama finally makes it to him.

The Queen personally informs Rama of his tragic fate with anxiety. Dasharath tries to refute it, but he is unable to. Rama turns to his father in the event that there is a miscommunication. Would only there were.

Rama evaluates the issue with majesty and objectivity. He reacts with wisdom. Well then, he responds. "I'm going to quit all I care about and spend 14 years in the Dandaka Forest. I'll also be going with a clear head.

Rama continues, "I am altering my plans—that I am going right now to embrace the woodland life of a mendicant. My father has made a commitment, and as his oldest son, it is my job to assist him fulfill it. But he worries about informing his mother since he believes she could pass away at the mere notion of being apart from him.

She first struggled to accept the news; she just won't listen to it, it's real. She insists on going with him to the forest while he continues to tell her the tale. He informs her that she is unable to depart and that she should stay at her husband's side to support him through this trying moment. She agrees grudgingly. The dreadful word quickly gets out. Men and women across the whole kingdom start sobbing vehemently.

Even though they wished to, they were unable to accompany Rama into exile. Several others really suggested going with him, but Kaikeyi forbade it since it would contradict the point of the exile if everyone entered the forest. There was just one chant heard in every house in Ayodhya since the people there loved Rama so much: "No! Dasharath shouldn't have approved of this at all! Yet Rama reassures them that there was no other option. Lakshman contends that Rama should not yield; in fact, he believes that Queen Kaikeyi's plot to install Bharata as king is the real motivation behind the whole tale of the boons promised. Lakshman is thus ready to wage war against his own family in order to restore Lord Rama.

Rama responds that following his father's instructions is the wisest course of action. Rama believed that breaking the news to Sita that he would now have to abandon her while keeping his vows in the jungle would be the most difficult aspect.

But it should come as no surprise that Sita, like so many other people in the realm, had no attachment to her opulent way of life: "If you go to the jungle," Sita replied, "I will walk ahead of you and make the route smooth by crushing the thorns beneath my feet. You won't be able to convince me to stay in your firm, and I won't leave.

Ramachandra, however, who is aware of the difficulties associated with life outside of Ayodhya, tells her about Dandaka's numerous prowling animals, crocodiles, and sharks in muddy rivers; how it is occasionally difficult to even get good drinking water—no bed, hunger satisfied only by fruits that fall to the ground, matted locks, bark for clothes, inclement weather, reptiles roaming free, pythons, Sita argues that she must remain with Rama no matter what, particularly during trying times, despite Rama's assertion that it is too risky.

Rama recalls that he had just advised his mother to remain with King Dasharath, which is the same counsel he now offers to his own mother. He now understands that Sita is right. Only by remaining at his side would she be able to discover the joy in life's trials; otherwise, even joys will seem terrible. It is obvious that she will not yield. Rama understands that he shares Sita's sentiments and that he could not stand to be apart from her for the same reasons.

As Rama and Sita are speaking, Lakshman, who is there, falls at his brother's feet because the idea of being apart makes him feel intolerable as well. One last time, Rama makes an effort to convince Sita and Lakshman not to go, but in vain.

Rama even attempts to persuade Lakshman to remain in the realm as a particular favor to him so that he may keep a close eye on the proceedings before the court. But Lakshman won't pay attention. He responds that Bharata can look after the kingdom, but he needs permission to accompany Bharata to the jungle. He would accompany Sita and Rama as their guide and get them food so they could enjoy the wilderness while he took care of all the grunt work.

Satisfied, the heavenly archer instructs Sita and Lakshman to get ready to leave right away. Dasharath passes away from sadness shortly after the gorgeous trio sets off on their quest. To accept his role as heir, young

THE HINDU EPICS – AN INTRODUCTION TO ANCIENT INDIA'S DEFINING MASTERPIECES.

Bharata is summoned back to Ayodhya. Before his mother, Queen Kaikeyi, welcomes him, Bharata finds out that his father has passed away and that his brother has been banished at his mother's request. With deep regret, Bharata accuses his own mother, Kaikeyi, of being a murderer.

Bharata believes that ascending to the throne without Rama and Lakshman is unthinkable. In other words, he opposes the proposal since he is Rama's brother and is a good and moral person. After conducting his father's burial ceremonies, Bharata leaves right away, followed by an army.

In addition to sending himself into exile in lieu of his older brother, he wants to bring Rama back. He believes that the only way he can possibly wash the stain of his mother's heinous act is by doing this.

After some time, Bharata and his army make their way to the area of Rama's woodland retreat. A soldier of his observes smoke coming from a cottage after climbing a tree.

So Bharata and a few others go on foot, and they soon see Rama's home. They enter and discover Rama's powerful bow, which has been gold-plated. Sharp arrows that are burning like the sun fill the quiver. There are gloves covered in gold and swords with golden sheaths.

In the middle of it all, Bharata notices a lotus-eyed Rama sitting on a black deerskin and sporting matted hair. They hug each other. Bharata informs him of Dasharath's death and begs Rama to come back and conquer his realm.

Rama is clearly upset by his father's sudden passing. But he responds philosophically, sharing with his younger brother his insights about the transience of the body and the enduring essence of the spirit. Rama encourages him to observe how people often welcome seasonal changes even if they signal the end of a person's physical and spiritual existence. He informs Bharata that death follows him and is ready to grab his pound of flesh whenever he goes for a simple stroll.

Because of this, says Rama, wise individuals can control their sadness. They continue living their lives with the knowledge that their loved ones have finished what they set out to do and have done so in accordance with God's will.

Bharata is instructed by Rama to go back to Ayodhya and assume leadership since their father had desired this. "Let me fulfill my responsibilities here," he says in conclusion. Bharata argues that Rama must oversee his authority since he is just a lad and that there is still much to be done.

Yet Rama is adamant on upholding his father's promise. Because of his brother's tenacity, Bharata decides to comply with his request but keeps a pair of Rama's sandals for himself. Following his return, he sets the sandals on an altar and makes a daily bow in front of them, allowing Rama to govern via his figurative presence. Bharata observes asceticism while he waits for the 14-year exile to end.

3 THE SLAYING OF RAVANA

As Rama and Sita, together with Lakshman, get used to living in the jungle, they encounter a variety of characters, both good and bad, and are involved in a number of exciting adventures. The renowned three spends their whole exile in either pleasure or danger in such exotic locations as the Dandaka Forest, the Panchavati Glade, and the Krauncha Jungle.

One of the dangerous meetings has deeper significance for their future: Shurpanakha, the demon's sister, is involved in an episode that sets off the fight with Ravana. A horrible witch-like creature named Shurpanakha wanders into Rama's hut and is overcome with desire when she sees the attractive prince. She starts to defame Sita and finally makes death threats. She does this in an effort to win Rama over and demonstrate her devotion to him. Instead, she simply incurs Lakshman's fury, who amputates her ears and nose. She runs back to Ravana's camp and begs for vengeance. But Ravana is more intrigued by his sister's depiction of Sita's beauty than by her own deformity. Yet, this is the first spark that ignites the War of Wars.

Ravana is a villain with an obsession for power who has almost everything. He has attained immense strength by the practice of rigorous penances and yogic discipline, including the previously mentioned special Lord Brahma boons.

He is the ruler of Lanka, a huge island nation, and he has almost limitless material luxury. He enjoys prowling through the jungle with his Rakshasa associates, slaying and devouring the flesh of isolated hermits engaged in spiritual activities. Early in his existence, Ravana was well known for raping attractive women without hesitation and assaulting them wherever he found them.

But a strong yogi had long ago cursed him, telling him that if he ever again tried to pleasure a woman via physical force, or, to put it another way, against her will, his skull would actually split in two.

In an effort to one day escape the curse, he now only brings wayward women back to his sizable harem of abused slaves. When he learns of Shurpanakha's suffering, he is furious because he believes that no one would dare to defy him in any manner. He sent 14,000 Rakshasa soldiers right away to kill Rama and Lakshman for their heinous act against his sister.

Nature attempts to warn Ravana's army along the way that they are entering holy ground by sending them a deluge of bad omens. Huge vultures attack their regal banners, frightening birds, monsters, and jackals cry, and blood rains from the heavens as black clouds reveal their ghastly shapes. The lovely horses hauling their chariots suddenly falter. Nonetheless, the Rakshasas still have a bloodlust. Rama is calm and collected despite being told of their impending arrival.

The arrows of Rama are glowing with beautiful hues, and his gold-plated bow seems to be vibrating with limitless energy, while disaster had been predicted for the Rakshasas by gloomy clouds and pouring blood. In addition to his gorgeous wife and the honorable Lakshman, he is surrounded by the numerous friends he has made throughout his time spent in the forest.

Rama defeats the 14,000 soldiers by himself and on foot in a fight that is fiercer than any other (despite the fact that many of his foes are riding chariots). His arrows blanket the whole sky, looking like blazing trees.

The Rakshasas have never faced a fighter of this caliber, and now it is obvious to them that their terrible lord will perish. One of them survives the battle and returns to Ravana to tell him that Ramachandra almost ate them up with his might. He said that everywhere they ran, Rama was waiting for them. Ravana is furious and warns the lone survivor that the cosmos will now experience his wrath, adding that even Vishnu had best go and hide. But the Rakshasa begs Ravana since he has just seen what Rama is capable of.

He warns him to beware of Rama's bravery and humbly concedes that Rama can use his arrows to raise the buried Earth from the depths of the ocean, bring down the stars and planets, and create new life from nothing.

He informs Ravana that Ramachandra cannot be overcome. The Rakshasa who survived adds that he had seen the lovely Sita. No woman, in his opinion, is as beautiful and admirable as she is. He explains to Ravana that she is young and the most elegant person he has ever seen. She is Rama's main treasure, the Rakshasa reasoned, and if Ravana could manage to divert him long enough to steal her, he would then be able to defeat him. After all, Rama could not stand to be separated from his beautiful bride.

Ravana accepts his servant's suggestion and moves on as planned. Ravana enlists the help of his warrior Maricha to kidnap Sita. Being the same Rakshasa who was propelled miles by Rama's wind shot when the heavenly 16-year-old had helped Vishvamitra earlier, this warrior had a score to clear with the Lord.

The strategy was now as follows: Maricha would playfully run-in front of Sita while assuming the shape of a golden deer (Rakshasas may alter their forms at whim). The heavenly princess will desire the deer for herself since she adores deer.

When Rama and Lakshman attempt to catch the deer at such time, Sita may be abducted by Ravana while they are attending to the animal. The strategy is promptly put into action. Maricha makes an amazing deer with silver markings and a jewel-like shine emerge in the woodland.

Sita is completely enthralled as it gallops in front of her and begs Rama to go out and catch it for her. Of course, Rama believes that

Maricha may be the culprit and that this is Rakshasa sorcery. As Sita requests, he chooses to pursue the deer, but if he is right about its identity, he would kill it. Rama admonishes Lakshman to safeguard Sita while he is away by staying behind with her. He chases the deer through the woodland as it runs away. It eventually becomes illusive, if not invisible. He decides to kill it since he is now confident that it is a Rakshasa disguised as a stunning deer. He draws his bow and fires a lethal arrow, which enters Maricha's heart like a burning serpent.

The Rakshasa's fictitious appearance vanishes, revealing him in his horrifying original shape, covered in blood and on the verge of death. Maricha, imitating Rama, yells out, "Sita!", as he draws his last breath. Lakshman! Aid me! Rama's heart sinks as soon as he hears this because he understands what is happening.

From her hut, Sita hears the demon's cry, and she is confident it is her devoted husband. She thinks the person she loves is in danger. She instructs Lakshman to assist him right away.

Yet, Lakshman rejects the notion that anything bad could happen to someone as magnificent as Rama. In addition, he is aware that he must stay to safeguard Sita. But the princess begs Lakshman to go since she is so worried about Rama, and he agrees.

Before departing, however, he creates a protective magical circle around their hut using Rama's name; if she would just remain within of it, it would protect her. Ravana disguises himself as an ascetic and approaches the hermitage to ask Sita for charity while Lakshman flees.

He asks Sita to kindly come outside since, as a monk, he is unable to enter a woman's house without another guy present. He draws her outside of Lakshman's circle, whereupon he transforms back into the dreadful Ravana and drags her away.

Ravana, the demon with 10 heads and twenty limbs, soars into the night on a massive, elaborate chariot known as the Pushpaka vimana (larger and more powerful than a contemporary jet) while clutching Sita as a spider snares a fly.

A devout devotee who has promised to defend the princess, the man-bird Jatayu, goes to her aid. But Ravana kills the enormous bird by severing his wings with his cruel sword. Following that, the villainous Ravana takes Sita to Lanka, his splendid country filled with sensuality and endless delights. It is stated that Sita's chasteness gives her protection from severe sexual misconduct and by the curse of Ravana.

Ravana wants to win Sita's heart because he can't satiate his passion. He gives her a tour of his lavish city, pointing out swans, ponds, and his harem of gorgeous ladies to demonstrate to her how lavishly his sex partners live.

He demonstrates to her how many powerful Rakshasas are eager to serve him and how they listen intently to whatever he says. He reassures her that she can have everything. Rama is disparaged by him as a helpless pariah who would never be able to enter Lanka's castle as he talks severely about him.

Ravana offers Sita the chance to govern over his luxurious realm while promising her that he will serve as her slave.

Despite her distress, she is able to tell him the truth: Rama and Lakshman will eventually destroy him because of his careless and provocative actions.

She continues, "How can the consort of a swan, one who games with her spouse among lotuses, love a water crow, who is wandering between weeds and bushes? ", in response to his threatening aggressiveness. I can no longer utilize this body. You may chain it or take it out. I won't give it a second thought going forward, and I'll never again be associated with unchaste women.

As a result, Ravana threatens her, saying, "Woman, if after one year you do not change your mind, I shall chop you into pieces and have my chefs serve you for dinner." She withdraws in disgust as Ravana has numerous servants lead her to her apartments.

Rama suffers intense anguish as a result of Sita's absence. He asks the trees and bowers if they have seen his love as he strolls around the forest wailing like a lunatic.

He worries that rakshasas have devoured his wife. Lakshman and he look around. Their lovely sylvan refuge is now devoid of color and vitality. Where has my sweetheart gone?" Rama asks the sun. He asks the wind whether she is living or dead and if he has ever seen her while on the road. Lakshman makes several arguments in an effort to cheer Rama up, but he is disregarded.

The brothers eventually discover evidence of Sita in the form of clothes that was ripped when she resisted Ravana and jewellery that had come off as she was taken away in his enchanted chariot.

Also, they discovered Jatayu's bleeding, lifeless corpse. It is important to remember that Jatayu made a heroic effort to stop Ravana from stealing Sita. In his last remarks, Jatayu warns Rama that Sita has been seized by

Ravana, Lord of the Rakshasas, and that he has personally seen this.

He also informs them that by collaborating with Sugriva, King of the Vanaras, they may get assistance in locating Ravana's land (who are a race of monkeys with humanlike characteristics).

Jatayu further tells them that the Vanaras reside in Pampa, a neighboring area characterized by rivers and lakes. They lament the departure of this committed person as Jatayu passes away in Rama's arms.

The two brothers carried out the last rites for the King of Birds and then promptly went in search of Sugriva. Sugriva's surveillance detects them coming in from a distance as they approach Pampa.

He and the Vanaras are hiding from his brother Vali, and Rama and Lakshman seem to be dangerous adversaries who may be going to fight on Vali's side, so he is afraid.

The monkeys go between peaks and swiftly

consult with their leader on what to do with the two powerful young men there.

Hanuman, the King's main advisor, informs Sugriva that Vali and his soldiers cannot be in Pampa since they would be refused entrance to the general region for a variety of complicated reasons. But why should Sugriva be afraid of these two fighters who resemble gods?

Hanuman approaches Rama and Lakshman on the king's behalf, certain that their worries are unfounded. He extends an invitation for them to meet the monkey chieftain with humility and eloquence.

Hanuman immediately catches Rama's attention, and he develops a deep fondness for him. They eventually set up a meeting with Sugriva. He sits down with the two brothers and they negotiate an agreement of honorable friendship. The monkey leader explains to Rama how he ended himself in Pampa and how he now fears for his life.

He was formerly the powerful king of

Kishkindha, but his ruthless brother Vali toppled him and abducted his wife. When Rama hears this, he thinks of Sugriva as a kindred soul who has gone through comparable adversity. He therefore consents to assist him in getting revenge on Vali. In return, the monkey leader vows to use his enormous Vanara army from all across the globe to assist Rama in saving Sita.

Sugriva, however, expresses skepticism on Rama's ability to defeat his wicked brother. After all, Vali is one of the most formidable fighters on the earth, and he is able to call upon troops that have undergone extensive training. Sugriva so requests that Rama demonstrate his skill as an archer.

To demonstrate his abilities to Sugriva, Rama fires one arrow that pierces through seven palm trees, a massive rock, and even the deepest part of the Earth. Then, all of a sudden, the arrow boomerangs back to Rama's quiver. There wasn't much else to be said. When Rama and Sugriva locate Vali, Sugriva and his brother engage in combat.

Rama unexpectedly ambushes Vali by shooting an arrow into his back at the most crucial time of their crucial fight. Rama thinks that this is the only way to get rid of this terrible perpetrator from the planet.

Ultimately, Vali dies, and Sugriva regains control of the kingdom of Kishkindha. The powerful monkey leader starts to gather his troops while maintaining his promise to Lord Ramachandra. Thousands of Vanaras are sent by him to look for Sita in Lanka. Yet, the soldiers start to lose faith after months of fruitless searches. Some go away, while others come back.

Ultimately, Hanuman learns that the kingdom of Lanka is located on an island far beyond the Indian Ocean, together with his companion Jambavan, a leader among the Vanara bears.

Despite the distance, Hanuman decides to go there on Rama's behalf and do research to determine if Sita is indeed being held hostage in Lanka. He can fly since he is the son of the wind deity Vayu. Like the Rakshasas, he possesses the capacity to alter form at will. Both abilities are beneficial, as we shall see.

Even for someone who can move like the wind, crossing the ocean is challenging. The monkey brothers of Hanuman assemble to bid him farewell. "I will reach Lanka with the velocity of the wind, exactly like an arrow launched by Rama, and if I do not find Sita there, I shall proceed to the domain of the gods at the same speed," he says to them as he leaps. He suddenly rises up and vanishes into the distance, saying, "And if I do not succeed even there, I will uproot Lanka itself and bring Ravana here in servitude.

Hanuman soars over the ocean like Garuda, the Eagle of Vishnu, causing enormous waves in his wake. The aquatic life forms stare up in awe as Hanuman passes by.

As he arrives at the beautiful city of Lanka, which is elaborate and seductive, he shrinks himself so that he may go around the city unnoticed. In the midst of Lanka's vibrant nightlife, Hanuman was thinking, "If I lose my life, significant hurdles would emerge in the completion of my master's purpose. He determines that it would be safer to stroll over rooftops, so he transforms into a cat and does so. He can make out the palace of Ravana, which is encircled by an enormous, shimmering wall, from a short distance away.

Hanuman carefully makes his way through boisterous bar crawls, enormous homes, and vibrant parks before reaching Ravana's residence. The palace seems to be its own city.

It floats in the sky like a massive spacecraft in the center of Lanka. Its beauty defies gravity and is unlike anything Hanuman has ever seen. Armed Rakshasas stand watch at the front gate.

The monkey warrior sees what seems to be a sea of beautiful ladies waiting for the Lankan lord to appear, it being far past midnight. Hanuman is focused on finding Sita despite being surrounded by such a bright harem. Yet his task is challenging since he has never really met her. At that very moment, he notices an ornately adorned bedstead positioned in the middle of Ravana's main room on a crystal dais. Ravana the lord was lying on the bed. He's sprawled over his silk sheets, drool trickling from his lips, and it's clear that he's drunk. His eyes are partially closed, and his body is covered with red sandal. He is the poster child for the sensualist in royal authority.

Where is Sita, though? She is not, thankfully, in Ravana's bedroom. Hanuman is still looking. She is eventually discovered by the honorable man-monkey sitting under a tree in the middle of the vast Ashoka Forest, which is connected to Ravana's domain.

Sita must be the person since she perfectly matches Rama's description. Even when compared to the most beautiful ladies in Ravana's court, her beauty is apparent. Tears stream down her cheeks as she is overcome with sadness yet remains bright.

She is referred to as "Lakshmi without the

Lotus," sitting on the ground like a hermit and sobbing for Rama's departure. Her days are spent being taunted by obscenely distorted Rakshasa creatures that dance in a ring around her and spread tales of Rama's frailty and demise. She often gets nighttime dreams about being separated from her lover.

Ravana visits her as Hanuman observes from a distance: "For ten months you have resisted my approaches. You still have two months remaining, the demon king informs. Hanuman cannot believe what he has heard, "After that I shall transform you into a pie and swallow you without a second thought."

On her part, Sita displays courage as Ravana talks. But as soon as he walks away, she collapses and begins to weep once again. The first thing Hanuman does is get in touch with her and tell her that Rama is safe.

In order to convince her that he is not another Rakshasa, he must gradually win her trust. Also, he wants to let her know that Rama and the Vanaras are on their way to save her. He starts to talk from behind the cover of the tree's branches. Sita is happy to hear his lovely voice, "I am sent by Rama." Despite her doubts, Hanuman is obviously not a monster. She hears him tell Ramachandra and King Dasharath's histories. Her heart expands when she hears these words.

Hanuman approaches her with great devotion and presents her with a ring that belonged to Rama and that she is used to. Hanuman received the ring from Rama expressly for this reason. She is now confident after seeing Rama's jewelry.

She removes a gem from her raven black hair and says, "Give this to Rama," in a joyful exchange. Hanuman chooses to assess the enemy's strength before returning with Sita's message, "And tell him to come immediately, else I shall definitely perish."

In an effort to be apprehended by Ravana's warriors, he causes a commotion in the hopes of being brought before the demon king.

Hanuman somehow destroys every tree in the Ashoka grove save from the one Sita is sitting under. Rakshasas run outside in terror as they see him growing enormously and aiming for the sky in a struggle.

Hanuman defeats hundreds of Rakshasa soldiers, including many of Ravana's senior military leaders, by himself during the onslaught. Ultimately, he consents to being taken into custody and is brought before Ravana. Their exchange is short. He is shackled from head to toe by Ravana. He sets the giant monkey warrior's tail on fire in an effort to further humiliate him. Hanuman, however, takes advantage of this humiliation to wreak havoc across the city. He enlarges himself even more and begins to soar between houses while lighting them on fire with his tail. He repeatedly declares: "None of you will live when you make Ramachandra your adversary!

Then he returns to the other side of the ocean and arrives among the Vanaras. They are happy as he shares the good news with them.

The Vanaras immediately mobilize under Sugriva and construct a miraculous stone bridge across the sea. With military hardware, literally millions march across the bridge and into Lanka.

Vanaras quickly take over the city, fighting Rakshasas and looking for Sita. Great heroes from both sides battle to the death in hand-to-hand combat, which results in thousands of deaths every day.

Great Rakshasa chieftains like Kumbhakarna, Narantaka, and Indrajit, the son of Ravana, eventually succumb to the indomitable might of heroes like Hanuman, Lakshman, Sugriva, and Ramachandra one by one. Vibhishana, Ravana's own brother, had already sided with Rama before to their invasion of Lanka.

He vowed to fight for everything right and decent since he could not stand his brother's bad actions. Today, much to Ravana's dismay, he battles valiantly for justice.

Lakshman is knocked out by Ravana's magical spear during one of the bloody fights against the Rakshasa army, and Rama reacts angrily: "If I lose the kingdom—this I can endure. Nevertheless, I can't handle losing Lakshman! If Lakshman dies, I can't continue!

Hanuman decides that only certain plants blooming in the Mountains can treat Lakshman after seeing him lying on the battlefield and declaring himself "horrified. As a result, the noble monkey flies to the well-known mountainous area in quest of the herbs while the combat is still in progress, moving like the wind itself. He has only a few seconds to do his work.

Moreover, the herbs are not to be found. As soon as he realizes he has to take action, he raises the whole mountain range and, while in the air, transports it back to the scene of the conflict, rescuing Lakshman just in time.

Rama uses a Brahmashtra that he releases from his bow to kill Ravana as the conflict comes to an end.

According to Valmiki, this sword was created and passed down from sage to sage by Lord

Brahma. As a result, the same Brahma who granted Ravana his blessing also provided the instrument that led to his death.

The Brahmashtra is an advanced weapon that uses a lot of power and produces smoke that looks like an apocalyptic fire. Ravana loses his life when Ramachandra shoots it, splitting Ravana's heart in two.

The final conflict is won, their commander dead, and the bulk of Rakshasas vanquished. Vibhishana, Ravana's religious brother, receives sovereignty of Lanka from Rama right after the battle.

Rama then goes back to Ayodhya. Everything seems to be going according to plan until Sita is presented to him. The wonderful couple had been apart for a while, and it had been a very difficult separation. Everyone anticipated that this would be a happy reunion.

But Rama declares that he cannot take Sita back since she has resided with Ravana in his home before the hordes of people arrive. This may seem like excessive conduct in the West, but in the East, such values are upheld with the utmost rigor.

Rama, who represents Vishnu in the human form, aspires to be the ideal human ruler and wants to lead by example.

Even though he has trust that Sita was entirely chaste throughout her time with the demon king Ravana, he rejects her in accordance with the mores and societal norms of the time.

A king's wife must be beyond reproach, and because in this instance some of his subjects may have doubts about her, he chooses to put her to the ultimate test.

Sita defends her virginity after hearing Lord Rama accuse her of it in front of the crowd. But the test has already been decided: Sita must enter a pure fire used for sacrifice. If she lives, she is also pure since Ravana has never touched her. She approaches the pyre and kneels down, pleading with the fire deity Agni for protection as the flames soar to enormous heights. She then bravely enters the flames. The most important of all the gods, Lord

Brahma, immediately descends from the heavens and asks Rama, "Why have you done this to Sita?

Agni emerges from the fire itself carrying Sita, who was fully uninjured because of her purity, while the question hangs in the air.

So, everyone in attendance could be certain that Sita had maintained her holiness despite having spent months with Ravana.

Yet years later, when Sita and Rama are in charge of a happy Ayodhya, Rama decides to exile his wife once again. His followers pick up where they left off with their criticism of her for spending time with Ravana.

Rama chooses to take advantage of their skepticism in order to enjoy "love in separation"; he urges her to endure yet another fire torture while knowing that it is unreasonable. Sita flees back to the ground, whence she originally originated, furious.

The inhabitants of Ayodhya eventually start to revere her and stop doubting her. But she has already made her way back to the planet.

Rama maintains a golden statue of his first wife at his side at all times and never takes another wife. No happy-ever-after here. He is reunited with her in all of his splendor after the span of his worldly life, when he returns to Ayodhya in the spiritual realm.

4 MAHABHARATA - THE BHARATA DYNASTY'S GREAT SAGA

The Mahabharata is the longest poem in history, and it is claimed to encompass all existential truths. Bharata refers to a significant patriarchal ruler of ancient India and his descendants, the people who helped to mold not just the future of Bharata's homeland but also, in some respects, the rest of the globe.

The adjective maha means "great" in Sanskrit. In terms of the text itself, Vyasa, the epic's fabled creator, asserts that he divided it into two parts: one ornate and one more succinct. In reality, according to legend, he wrote a version with six million stanzas, of which three million are known to those in the celestial sphere, one and a half million to the ancestors, one million and four hundred thousand to the angels, and just a thousand to those in the human world. The current version, albeit the critical edition is obviously a little bit shorter, supports this final number.

The Mahabharata covers a wide range of topics in its extensive chapters, with innumerable asides and subplots. Yet its main story is on the ferocious conflict between the related cousin clans, the Pandavas and the Kauravas, who ruled over 5,000 years ago. A full-scale civil war breaks out between gods and humans, Brahmins and aristocracy, and even Krishna, the Ultimate Being.

The vast amount of astronomical, archeological, and literary evidence has led experts to the conclusion that the battle recounted in the Mahabharata really took place about 3102 BCE. Its primary battleground was in the present-day Indian state of Haryana, but it also had several colonies elsewhere.

Although some academics dispute whether the war truly occurred, the majority agree that it happened, albeit in a somewhat condensed version. Of fact, traditionalists and several practitioners swear to its validity, insisting that its supernatural aspects are a normal aspect of God's earthly amusements. King Dhritarashtra, the father of the Kauravas, is introduced as the protagonist of the tale.

While he should have been entitled to the throne by right as the older brother of the royal family, his blindness prevents him from assuming it. Instead, it is handed to his younger brother Pandu, the father of the Pandavas (Yudhishthira, Arjuna, Bhima, Nakula, and Sahadeva—all of whom were miraculously conceived), in line with Vedic law. Pandu's ascension to the throne infuriates Dhritarashtra, who never forgets it.

Pandu died young, and Dhritarashtra took in his five sons, the Pandavas, and raised them alongside his own sons, the Kauravas, the oldest of which was Duryodhana, at his court. As Pandu's oldest child, Yudhishthira was now the legitimate successor to the kingdom. Dhritarashtra was enraged by this since handing up the kingship to Pandu was challenging enough. Duryodhana, the son of Dhritarashtra, would now have to cede the throne to Yudhishthira and the Pandavas, adding salt to injury. All the lads get Kshatriya (warrior) training in accordance with age-old ideals of valor and chivalry that are now all but forgotten.

Rivalry grew between the Kauravas and the Pandavas even while they were still little kids. Actually, it all started with Duryodhana's enmity towards the Pandavas and their legitimate position as kings. But eventually, it developed farther. The Pandavas become kind; the Kauravas turned cunning. As they age, the Kauravas abuse their military power for personal gain, but the Pandavas are revered because they are spiritual political leaders.

Although though it is becoming obvious that the Pandavas are more qualified to lead the realm, Dhritarashtra still naturally prefers his own sons and manages to arrange the enthronement of his oldest son, Duryodhana. The sons of Pandu finally get their own area, where they build a massive metropolis. Duryodhana, however, is envious and devises a scheme to seize the Pandavas' territory by questionable methods. He arranges a dice game so that Yudhishthira, the oldest son of Pandu, would undoubtedly lose. Yudhishthira loses his kingdom as a result of the plot's success, and the Pandavas are exiled for 13 years.

The Pandavas were ideal Kshatriyas, just as Rama had been many millennia previously when he had personified the Kshatriya spirit. Because of their Kshatriya nature, they accept their unfair loss and enter the jungle with the hope of regaining their kingdom when they emerge.

But, Duryodhana refuses them the kingdom that is rightly theirs after 13 years (during which they have forest adventures that, once again, are reminiscent of those in the Ramayana). They then request five tiny villages since it is their desire and duty as Kshatriyas to dominate. Moreover, it is essential for their survival. Duryodhana is ruthless, nevertheless.

Instigating what was to become a catastrophic struggle with his demeaning retort and unwillingness to allow them even minor settlements, he sneers, "If they want as much land as fits under a pin, they will have to fight for it." Even though there is still a chance that the battle may be stopped, the Kauravas seal their destiny by trying to strip off Draupadi, the Pandavas' wife, in front of everyone. Krishna saves her by providing an endless supply of fabric to cover her body.

Duhshasana, a prominent Kaurava tyrant, tugs at her clothing to the same extent that fresh fabric mystically arises. Nevertheless, it is already too late for the Kauravas; no amount of fabric could keep the Pandavas from seeing the humiliation and the declaration of impending war. At this point, the Kauravas had earned a reputation as rapacious monarchs. As previously mentioned, the Mahabharata identifies the five sons of Pandu as manifestations of heavenly personalities (Adi-parvan 109.3).

Duryodhana, however, is seen as the Kali Purusha—the demon Kali in human form (Adi 61.80). He represented conflict and hypocrisy, in other words, everything that was wrong with society. He shows signs of who he is by mistreating the Pandavas and everyone else in the realm. By any definition, he and the Kauravas are "evil-doers."

Vedic law holds that they are responsible for six offenses that call for fatal retaliation:

(1) giving poison;

(2) setting fire to another's house;

(3) stealing;

(4) seizing another's property;

(5) snatching another's wife; and

(6) assaulting with a deadly weapon.

The Kauravas repeatedly stole the Pandavas'

land; they kidnapped Draupadi (when they attempted to strip her); and now, with war imminent, they are about to attack them with the deadliest of weapons. Duryodhana had fed Bhima, the strongest of the Pandava boys, a poisoned cake in one of several attempts to kill him. He had also ordered the construction of a lacquer house for the Pandavas and then set it on fire while they and their mother

According to Vedic literature, such assailants or offenders (atatayi) should be put to death by guardians of the virtuous. If he be a teacher, the Manu-Samhita 8.350-1 states: ". . . If he appears as a criminal (atatayi) in any of the six ways mentioned above, a Kshatriya should kill him, even if he is an elderly or well-educated Brahmin.

Similarly, the Pandavas were not the only victims of the Kauravas' hatred; Hindu tradition claims that "such a criminal is in truth murdering himself by his own outrageous actions" rather than that "there is no fault in killing one so cruel." The Kauravas' oppressive rule spread across the nation as it developed, bringing chaos and suffering for all of their victims. Therefore, the Pandavas' retaliation wasn't motivated by vengeance but by a desire to protect their fellow humans.

On summarizing the Kauravas' rule during the Pandava exile, Professor Pandit Rajmani Tigunait quotes from the Mahabharata as follows: "During this time of exile, the false king and his sons assembled a large military force, stored weapons, and established agreements with surrounding kingdoms." Their people were suffering; taxes were high, and every dollar went toward building up the army; corruption was rife; and women and children were not protected. They prayed for the exiled legitimate monarch and his four brothers to return.

When they did, the legitimate monarch sent an ambassador to the court with a plan for regaining control of his realm. The idea was rejected, and the ambassador was abused. The Pandavas seeks peace, which should be emphasized. The Mahabharata meticulously records this information.

Furthermore, the Udyoga-Parvan recalls a number of moments in which both Krishna and the Pandavas beg for an end to the folly that lay before them; strangely, this book is known as "the Book of Effort" and highlights the enormous effort made by the Pandavas to avert the conflict. Yet despite how sincere they are, none of these petitions are granted. Battle then breaks out since there are no other options.

The Yadavas were being led by Lord Krishna, who the cousins referred to as God incarnate, who was from the glorious city of Dvaraka on the western coast of India. He pledges himself, along with his whole army, to the oncoming conflict. Therefore, neither side may have both; they must choose one or the other.

Krishna made it clear that he would not fight; whomever picks him would have to be satisfied with his moral support. He will drive the chariot as well. The opposite side could have his practically infinite armies of skilled fighters. Materialistic Duryodhana selects the armed troops with little delay. On the other side, the good Pandavas request just Krishna, believing that God's favour is more important than any material comfort.

According to the Mahabharata, Krishna demonstrates the objectivity of God by allowing each side choose whether to use his army or himself. If someone turns to Him, He responds appropriately; if they choose worldly comforts, He gives them everything they ask for in line with their karma. The decisions taken here by the Pandavas and Duryodhana, respectively, show the real cause of the Mahabharata war: It was ultimately not about giving the Pandavas the territory they were denied, but rather about building a monarchy that was God-conscious.

As we have seen, Duryodhana had no interest in becoming aware of God. The Kauravas did not wish to reign on behalf of Krishna, but the Pandavas did. According to indologist Angelika Malinar, the Udyoga-parvan depicts a series of dialogues on the advantages and disadvantages of war, Yudhishthira's claim to be king, and Duryodhana's attempt to establish himself as an absolute ruler. He and his supporters provide clever justifications for their demands for an "absolute" administration that is oriented on the king's interests.

Duryodhana, despite the cautions of those in positions of power, is adamant about establishing his dominance over the three realms, including gods and demons. . . to put his own self-interest ahead of the customary family bonds and the ethic of kinship. He positions himself as a god-king and rejects all commitments to the old gods as well as to ascetic, or self-restrictive, ideals in his thematic speech in the Mahabharata (5.60).

So, the Pandavas have no choice but to engage in combat in order to protect the just and build a country that is aware of God. The Bhagavad-Gita, which is the first chapter of the sixth book of the Mahabharata, starts out with Krishna acting as Arjuna's charioteer. What really happened to cause the Gita to be recited may be summed up as follows. Both forces are positioned and prepared for battle. Krishna, however, maneuvers Arjuna's chariot towards the center of the conflict before the combat starts. The famous bowman encounters friends, family members, and other countrymen there on both sides. He gets gripped by terror and has second thoughts about joining the enormous battle that is about to begin—a conflict in which no one can really win. Krishna then starts to speak—or, more accurately, to sing.

The Bhagavad-Gita is this. Arjuna asks Krishna his inquiries in an attempt to end his existential predicament, which is how the Gita's song is presented as a conversation. The intricate philosophical concepts that emerge from this very affecting conversation cover a wide variety of topics, including the soul and life after death, material nature and how it affects human psychology, and an explanation of the essence of God.

The Bhagavad-Gita will be covered in-depth in the next chapter. Let it be known for the time being that Arjuna is prepared to battle and is relieved, if not enlightened, by the Gita's conclusion. Strong troops may be seen on both sides of the battlefield as Arjuna takes up his choice. In addition to the large armies, there are countless smaller forces from other nations. The Pandavas succeed in assembling a military army that is often divided into seven major divisions.

The Kauravas had assembled a far greater army made up of eleven such divisions, which, although threatening, is still not insignificant. Each of these divisions included 21,870 chariots, an equivalent number of elephants, three times as many cavalries, and five times as many foot warriors, according to modern Mahabharata experts.

The Pandavas had 153,090 chariots and an equivalent number of elephants in their army, together with 459,270 riders and 765,450 warriors. 240,570 chariots and elephants, 721,710 horsemen, and more over 1 million warriors make up the Kauravas' army.

According to tradition, this is a low estimate,

indicating that many millions of people were really murdered in the conflict. Regardless of how the numbers are calculated, unfathomably enormous forces are converging on this battlefield to engage in combat. In fact, a global war is often used to characterize it.

According to Linda Johnsen, an authority on Hinduism, the fight depicted in the Mahabharata might be considered the real First World War. Participants included soldiers from Greece and Indonesia.

When one considers that India throughout the most of history represented one of the richest and most intelligent civilizations in the world, this is not that shocking.

Sailors from European nations were frantically looking for passages to India as late as 400 years ago. Control of some of the most significant trade routes in the globe was at stake in the conflict between Duryodhana and Arjuna's brother.

Archaeological finds like those at Mohenjo-

Daro show that northern India was a sophisticated, multiracial region visited and inhabited even thousands of years before the advent of Christ.

According to the book, the battle claimed the lives of hundreds of thousands of people. First fighting is conducted in accordance with Kshatriya protocol, which stipulates that only daylight should be used for conflict.

All of the soldiers mingle in friendliness in the evening. Only equals engage in one-on-one combat. Soldiers who are simply on foot are not attacked by horsemen. Chariot warriors only engage in combat with other chariot warriors. Both those sitting in a yoga position and anyone withdrawing for any other reason are not targeted.

Musicians, conch blowers, and civilians—all are immune to the surrounding warfare—are left alone if someone drops their weapon. Animals are never intentionally murdered, but if they do so accidentally during a conflict, it is ignored.

Yet, like in all battles, as emotions rise and the struggle approaches its conclusion, these guidelines are completely undermined. How the principles of dharma, of righteous obligation, could be so misapplied on the battlefield while Krishna himself was there has been questioned by many.

Nonetheless, it must be recognized that Krishna's goal was for this dharmic misuse to occur. It was a necessary evil that made room for the full manifestation of dharma's real value. Interesting is how this appears specifically.

The three phases of the Mahabharata battle show the emergence of dharma first, when Arjuna recognizes the virtue in defending a just cause; then, its inevitable compromise, as when the Kshatriya ethical precepts break down on the battlefield; and finally, the reestablishing of dharma manifests in the conclusion, when Krishna, according to the legend, saves the Pandava clan from extinction, reestablishing cosmic order once more. Let's elaborate on this a little. Noble motivations led to the start of the conflict.

After that, though, mindless devastation takes over. Shiva's presence on the battlefield is largely responsible for this. That is to say, as per Krishna's design, of course, the lord of devastation brings his own brand of dharma to the battlefield. What causes this to occur? Shiva himself arrives and causes mayhem on the thirteenth day of a conflict that will endure for 18 days (each horrific day is recounted below).

He also makes an appearance in the form of Ashvatthama, who is the target of a lot of scheming in the closing stages of the conflict, as we will see.

Moreover, he directs a nocturnal slaughter in which he murders the majority of the Pandavas' unborn offspring. Shiva accomplishes his goals by playing out what Krishna refers to as fated events, which includes the killing of many fighters.

Dharma therefore emerges and is subsequently almost completely destroyed. In the end, however, Krishna steps in to save one of the Pandava grandsons, Pariksit, shielding the infant from Ashvatthama while it is still within its mother.

The Puranas, the apex of Indian spiritual literature, which will be covered in the chapter following this, include several references to Pariksit. Yet we take things too far. The blind King Dhritarashtra watches the battle from behind the lines drawn by the Kauravas as his minister Sanjaya relates everything to him.

5 BATTLES OF THE GREAT WAR

On Day 1 of the 18-day battle known as "The Battle of Battles," it seems like the Pandavas may lose. Grandson of the clan and heroic general Bhishma finds himself on the side of the Kauravas. He engages in combat with Arjuna's son Abhimanyu and, as a result of his maturity and experience, wins.

Along with fighting for the Pandavas, Uttara, an Arjuna relative, also attacks Shalya, the Kaurava prince who is Madri's brother and the uncle of Nakula and Sahadeva. Uttara accidently kills Shalya's horse in the middle of the conflict, which infuriates him and makes him fight more fiercely. As a result, he murders Uttara, the first battle fatality, dealing the Pandava princes a severe blow. Shortly after, Shveta, a warrior from the Pandava family, strikes back against Shalya and uses his exceptional aim to take on the whole Kaurava army.

Yet when he confronts Bhishma, he is eventually put to death. When the first day comes to an end, the Pandavas are thus not very optimistic. The Pandava top commander, Dhrishtadyumna, positions his troops in a tactical posture as the sun rises on the second day.

Grandsire Bhishma thwarts the majority of the Pandavas' intentions, despite the fact that the Pandavas benefit from this and do better than they did on the first day. It is difficult for Arjuna to agree that the grandsire must be killed since Bhishma is a highly esteemed fighter, a senior family member, and a teacher who has taught Arjuna and the others much of what they know.

Arjuna, however, strikes the noble grandsire with tenacity and prowess. Because to the fact that he is one of their prize warriors, the Kauravas make an effort to keep him safe. Arjuna is forced to fight them off, which causes him to lose focus on his main goal of killing Bhishma.

In the excitement of battle, Bhishma shoots an arrow at Krishna, who is now serving as Arjuna's charioteer. Arjuna is quite upset by this, but he can't yet capture Bhishma. Arjuna is particularly enraged by Drona's support for the Kauravas in their battle. Drona is a significant spiritual figure who served as the major instructor of both the Pandavas and the Kauravas as well as Ashvathama's father. Yet a complicated chain of circumstances made this inevitable.

Consequently, on the second day, we see Drona battling the Pandava general Dhrishtadyumna, who almost perishes as a consequence of Drona's actions. Then Dhrishtadyumna is saved by Bhima, who rescues him on his chariot. Thereafter, Duryodhana sends several warriors in pursuit of Bhima, who kills them one by one.

Even though the attack is just on Day 2, the battle has already become much worse. The Kauravas are compelled to back off when the day eventually comes to a close, which makes them feel relieved.

On Day 3, Arjuna is being attacked by several Kaurava troops at once. He manoeuvres them away with amazing dexterity. Shakuni, the principal advisor to Duryodhana, lunges for Satyaki, a significant Pandava warrior. Even though Abhimanyu's chariot is wrecked in the process, he is ultimately successful in saving him.

Both Drona and Bhishma pursue Yudhishthira in the hope of killing the oldest Pandava brother and swiftly winning the battle. They fall short, however. Bhishma receives a reprimand from Duryodhana for not fighting well. The Pandavas are compelled to flee for their life when Bhishma's ferocious assault on them infuriates him.

Even while he battles the Pandavas and their supporting soldiers, Bhishma never stops praising them. He feels humiliated to go up against people who are so moral. He reduces the force of his onslaught, giving the advantage back to the Pandavas.

The Kauravas are on the run at the end of the day. Yet on the fourth day, Bhishma, Drona, and Duryodhana battle like men driven by a maniacal urge, helping the Kauravas advance their cause once again. Abhimanyu is being surrounded by many Kaurava soldiers who are preparing to murder him. Then Arjuna, his father, steps in to save him. At that very moment, Dhrishtadyumna shows up with more troops, including the formidable Bhima.

The Kauravas send out a big troop of elephants to defeat this unstoppable behemoth that had almost single-handedly destroyed them the day before. Nevertheless, Bhima is able to disperse the elephants, which causes dread and panic among the Kaurava army. He also strikes Duryodhana, almost killing him, by capitalizing on the disarray. Remarkably, the wicked Kaurava manages to compete with this very talented Pandava and ultimately triumphs. But, Ghatotkacha, the son of Bhima, is able to save him before Duryodhana strikes a fatal blow. Bhima murders eight of Duryodhana's brothers after being revived.

At dusk, the Pandavas have achieved a momentary win, and the Kauravas are in a terrible state of despair.

On the fifth day, the Pandavas come close to winning the whole conflict. While battle starts with Bhishma conducting a well-thought-out assault on the Pandavas, inflicting tremendous destruction and almost decimating many of their key warriors, Arjuna leads a reaction that comes close to matching the harm caused by Bhishma.

Duryodhana laments to Drona about his men's frailty because he can't stand their ineptitude. Next, Drona attacks Satyaki in the hope that the loss of such a skilled general would act as a leveler. Then Bhima steps in to save him, shielding him from Drona's blow. The brave sons of Satyaki are now killed.

Arjuna himself slaughters thousands of Kaurava troops after reacting angrily. The day comes to a successful conclusion for the Pandavas.

Day six is a day of widespread genocide. Many warriors are killed in the process. Arrows were everywhere, and blood covered the ground. In an intriguing side scene, Bhima boldly engages in a one-on-one battle with eleven of Duryodhana's best men. He becomes trapped behind Kaurava lines during this conflict, and Dhrishtadyumna heroically tries to rescue him. The Kauravas assault the two Pandava warriors when they are on enemy territory. When he is surrounded, Dhrishtadyumna utilizes a supernatural weapon that Drona gave to him while he was a student and that he had received when he was very young. The weapon's mental effects render the user unconscious.

As a consequence, the Kauravas are pacing aimlessly, as if they are drunk. But when Duryodhana shows there, he uses a similar weapon and knocks the Pandavas to the ground. The effects of the weapons eventually wear off as the soldiers make their way out of the afflicted region. The Kauravas are said to have won the day. There are several one-on-one fights once again on the seventh day.

Several of Duryodhana's trained troops perish, more on the Kaurava side than the Pandava side.

Each of the five Pandava princes feels proud to be up against such a worthy foe as Bhishma, who takes on all five of them by himself. While some warriors battle bravely, the dead just pile up. The destruction is unheard of.

After sundown, evening meals are replaced with wound care.

On the eighth day of the war, Bhima obliterates eight of Duryodhana's brothers. On the same day, Iravat, one of Arjuna's sons, is murdered. While emotionally broken, Arjuna continues to fight. Ghatokacha successfully attacks the Kauravas. In a heartwarming moment, Duryodhana strikes out expertly but almost perishes; he is saved just in time by Drona. On that day, sixteen of Dhritarashtra's sons are put to death. Grandsire Bhishma kills a great number of Pandava soldiers on the ninth day.

The only way to win the battle, according to Krishna, is for Arjuna to go above and beyond to eliminate Bhishma. Arjuna, however, once again lacked the willpower to murder his former instructor. Infuriated, Krishna gets from the chariot and proceeds to fight Bhishma directly on foot. Then Arjuna yanks him back. Arjuna would take the appropriate action when the moment came, and Krishna was not to engage in direct combat.

As the day goes on, Satyaki and Ashvatthama engage in combat, and Drona and Arjuna. These 24 hours are mostly in the Kauravas' advantage. Bhishma's accident the next day, however, paints a different picture. Arjuna successfully engages him with a barrage of arrows, leaving him gravely wounded.

On an arrowhead cushion, the Grandsire slowly perishes. He considers Arjuna killing him an honor. The most renowned of all noble warriors receives greetings from the demigods who have traveled from beyond the universe.

In reality, the fighting stops for a moment as both sides honor the senior-most individual who had instructed them all.

As Bhishma requests for water, Arjuna answers by shooting an arrow into the earth, which causes water to pour into his teacher's mouth and rise into the sky. Bhishma preaches the necessity for peace while lying on his deathbed on the battlefield. He lives for 58 days thanks to his yogic abilities, which he uses to prolong his life so that he might pass away during the sun's northern phase and, in doing so, achieve perfection in death.

He talks philosophically throughout this period, and his words are recorded in the Mahabharata, the Bhagavata, and other Puranas. The Grandsire continues to give lectures for the rest of his 58 days after the 18-day war is over.

The Kauravas make the decision to capture Yudhishthira alive while the battle continues. Drona enthusiastically accepts the proposal as soon as Duryodhana comes up with it, mostly because he does not want to see Yudhishthira murdered.

The main reason Duryodhana wants to capture the main Pandava is to mislead him into playing another game of chance. Nevertheless, the other Pandavas quickly learn of the scheme and make preparations to foil it.

The next day, Drona makes an effort to carry out her plot to kidnap Yudhishthira. But, the great Pandava prince escapes on horseback; while a real Kshatriya would never flee from another Kshatriya, Yudhishthira justifies doing so since Drona is actually a Brahmana and it is not dishonorable to do so.

As this is going on, Sahadeva and Shakuni, the maternal uncle of the Kauravas, engage in violent one-on-one fight.

On this day, several great warriors compete at their very best: Shalya vs. Nakula, Dhrishtaketu vs. Kripa, Satyaki vs. Kritavarman, and Virata vs. Karna. Abhimanyu engages in simultaneous duels with four skilled Kauravas and fights like a maniac.

Drona attempts to catch Yudhishthira once again after seeing him in the distance. Nevertheless, Arjuna blocks the route, causing Drona to back off. The Kauravas are having a terrible day on their eleventh, and many of their soldiers start to lose motivation.

During the 12th day, the Kauravas understand that Arjuna's presence would prevent them from capturing Yudhishthira. So, they come up with a scheme to murder him. Our unprepared Pandava hero is attacked by Susharman and his four brothers. Yet he is able to kill them because to his unerring Kshatriya instinct. Drona makes another attempt to kidnap Yudhishthira when the plot to assassinate Arjuna falls through. Once again, he is unable to do so because Dhrishtadyumna and his allies are waiting nearby to defend him. The chief Pandava is constantly attempted to be abducted by the Kauravas, but each time they fail.

Only a few feet away, there are other beautiful conflicts going on. For instance, Abhimanyu, the son of Arjuna, is encircled by Kaurava troops. He holds his own against the whole Kaurava army, including Duryodhana, in a titanic display of bravery. The other Pandavas make an effort to help him, but they are unable to even approach. The Kauravas focus all of their energy on him. He eventually uses nothing but a chariot wheel to fend them off, swinging it crazily.

Ultimately, Lakshman, the son of Duhshasana, kills him with a single, powerful stroke. Yuyutsu, one of Dhritarashtra's sons, is so shocked by the deceit that he puts down his sword and flees the battlefield. Many people on both sides are saddened at how Abhimanyu is slain. The fight still goes on.

On the thirteenth day, Arjuna kills a large number of Kaurava troops before facing Duhshasana, a significant Kaurava prince who, in many respects, was the main instigator of the conflict. He is overcome by Arjuna, and he escapes.

As a symbol of a little triumph, Arjuna blows his conch at this moment. The Pandavas engage in combat like never before. Particularly Bhima is fighting the Kauravas like toy soldiers, sending their corpses flying in all four directions. Shiva is there, however, and this changes the mood and tenor of the whole conflict.

Several of the key fighters are worn out by the fourteenth day. A small kingdom's prince, Bhurishravas, lifts his sword against Satyaki, king of the Vrishnis (vital Pandava allies), and kills him while sparring with him. While engaged in a battle with another foe some distance away and seeing Satyaki's struggle, Arjuna manages to unleash a hail of arrows in the direction of Bhurishravas, severing his right arm. Bhurishravas concedes defeat, resolves to end the conflict, and then starts to practice yoga while still engaged in combat, sitting in the lotus position.

As Satyaki notices this, he becomes enraged and immediately beheads Bhurishravas, which is obviously wrong. Both sides are now disregarding the laws of war as their desire for blood drives them to do whatever it takes to prevail. Arjuna engages Jayadratha, a significant Kaurava ally, in a fierce combat before turning to deception.

Arjuna beheads Jayadratha with a stream of arrows that carry the head into the lap of his father, who is meditating nearby. Jayadratha's father had made a prediction, or, rather, a curse: "Whoever causes my son's head to fall to the ground will find that his own will burst into a hundred pieces." Krishna informs Arjuna of this curse.

Being disturbed from concentration, the father gets out of bed and unintentionally lets his son's head fall to the floor. His skull explodes into fragments as his own curse requested since he is the one who directly caused the boy's head to hit the ground. After this, the fight rages on into the night with the aid of torches, directly violating the laws of war.

On the evening of the fifteenth day, the majority of Kshatriya ethical norms have been abandoned. Even Krishna breaks the rules of knightly conduct to aid the Pandavas. He advises murdering the elephant after giving it the name Ashvatthama, which is also the name of Drona's kid. The plan is to inform Drona that "Ashvatthama" has passed away so that he would believe he has lost his son and, in consequence, give up on life altogether. Then it would be simple to beat him. The strategy is carried out, but as Drona is aware that Yudhishthira is truthful at all times, she chooses to get her approval. Yudhishthira announces to the whole battlefield that Ashvatthama was, in fact, dead.

A side note: According to conventional Hindu belief, King Yudhishthira had to visit hell because he lied on behalf of Krishna and said, "Ashvatthama is dead," but the Vaishnava tradition teaches that he went to hell because he hesitated to speak that falsehood. The tradition holds that even while ordinary morality is seen as obligatory in all other situations, God's will takes precedence over it. In other words, one should only do so if God Himself is physically there and commands the suspension of worldly ethics, as He did with Yudhishthira. If not, it is a sin.

It was true that Ashvatthama "the elephant" had passed away, as Yudhishthira had genuinely said. In order to make Drona believe that his son had died, Krishna purposefully drowned out the words "the elephant" with the sound of his conch at that precise time. As a result, Drona laid down his weapons and was instantly beheaded by Dhrishtadyumna. The strategy so succeeded. The surviving Pandavas and Kauravas could now see the agony of battle and how even the most virtuous Kshatriyas may be transformed into opportunistic automaton with no purpose other than the drive to triumph at any costs. Karna assumes command of the Kaurava army upon the passing of Drona.

Yet few people really want to fight. Karna challenges Yudhishthira to a duel on the sixteenth day, and the two engage in battle for a while. The battle reaches its peak, but Yudhishthira escapes, unwilling to continue the pointless fighting with those he cares about.

Bhima, on the other hand, is unafraid and strikes Duhshasana after recalling Draupadi's humiliation when the Kauravas tried to strip her of her clothing. Bhima's defeat of this dreadful Kaurava bandit, who tore apart his body with his own hands, is perhaps one of the most memorable, though unsettling, moments in the whole Mahabharata conflict.

While the soldiers on both sides are horrified by Bhima's unyielding behavior, they all agree that Duhshasana, being the rascal that he was, could not but meet a terrible end. Arjuna and Karna engage in a difficult and protracted combat on the seventeenth day. Despite their heroic efforts, Arjuna finally prevails, although in a contested manner.

In fact, Yudhishthira chastises him for how the war is won. But Arjuna is not about to listen to his older brother, who had already fled in disgrace. He is furious that his brother would question him, and he plans to slash Yudhishthira with his sword in retaliation. The brothers, however, are brought to reason by Krishna's intervention.

All Kaurava soldiers are under Shalya's leadership after Karna's death, and they are aware that the battle is about to finish. Notwithstanding their internal conflicts, the Pandavas come together and triumph for the sake of dharma on the 18th and last day of the fight.

In the end, Duryodhana is essentially alone himself. As he realizes he has lost, he flees and hides in a nearby lake using a mysterious power that allows him to stay underwater for protracted periods of time.

Sahadeva defeats Shakuni and Yudhishthira kills Shalya, two significant losses for the Kaurava army as he vanishes.

The surviving sons of Dhritarashtra are then killed by Bhima, with the exception of Duryodhana, who is still submerged. But he locates the last Kaurava leader's hiding location in the lake and looks for him. He drags Duryodhana outside while taunting him. They continue to engage in combat while using enormous clubs as the demon king emerges from the lake.

After shattering both of his legs with a last blow below the belt, Bhima tramps over the man's torso. Yudhishthira smacks Bhima across the face in response to his ire at this unjust and cruel behavior.

Krishna's brother Balarama, who is absent for the most of the battle but shows up just in time to see Bhima acting dishonestly, is so outraged that he assaults Bhima with his plow (Balarama's preferred weapon). He and his brother both go towards the Pandavas' capital city of Dvaraka when Krishna, who has sympathy for the Pandavas, stops him.

The still-alive Duryodhana criticizes Krishna as he moves along, but no one pays attention as the voice of the now-paralyzed demon grows progressively quieter; the others leave, and Duryodhana passes away.

The conflict has ended. The original five Pandavas, their commander Satyaki, and of course Krishna, are all still alive. The last remaining Kaurava warriors are Kripa, Ashvatthama, and Kritavarma. All of the Pandavas' offspring have been slaughtered, with the exception of Arjuna's future monarch Pariksit.

The principal warriors' remains are collected, draped in fragrant linen, placed on a huge funeral pyre, and burned.

While Yudhishthira is crowned King of Hastinapura, everyone is concerned about the cost of the battle. At least Dhritarashtra is confident that it is not worth losing all of his sons. He gives Yudhishthira a hug in an effort to promote harmony and peace. But, when Bhima is shown to the blind king, Krishna substitutes a metal statue for him, which Dhritarashtra shatters out of rage.

The Pandavas are blessed despite Dhritarashtra and his wife's inability to pardon them since they are aware of the justice of their cause.

Hastinapura's ruler, Yudhishthira, harbors resentment against the conflict and the countless lives it claimed. He is aware that he and his brothers must pay a price by spending some time in physical hell, and the Mahabharata does indeed detail their voyage there. But later, they become godlike and enter Krishna's heavenly dwelling.

6 LESSONS OF THE EPICS

What lessons do Hindus learn from these massive texts? The stories of the Mahabharata and the Ramayana feature many morals and rules of behavior that have directed people for millennia and have filled volumes of literature. Smaller books have also been taken from the Epics, including the Bhagavad-Gita, the Vishnu-Sahasranam, Bhishma's teachings, Nala and Damayanti's love story, Shakuntala's story, Sita's story, and Hanuman's exploits, all of which contain in-depth philosophical guidance that promotes virtue and a religious way of life. Given this, it may seem a little odd that both Epics are focused on battle and include military themes, seemingly advocating murder as a reasonable reaction to injustice.

Nonetheless, very few Hindus would assert that this is the main theme of the Epics. Instead, they believe that the primary lesson that emerges is dharma, or obligation. They claim that when practiced correctly, dharma gives tranquility and contentment. And when carried out to the fullest extent under the guidance of a spiritual master, it results in emancipation and the love of God. Most Hindus believe that this is the main message of both the Ramayana and the Mahabharata.

It's interesting to note that according to the Epics, dharma is the highest virtue and exists for the benefit of everybody. Moreover, they advocate nonviolence toward God's creations as one of the purest forms of dharma.

Nonviolence is the ultimate duty and the highest instruction, according to the Mahabharata (13.116.37–41), however things are not always so straightforward. Why do the Epics wave their peace flag from a violent battlefield if they promote the qualities of peaceful contact, as they do?

Again, the term dharma, which is uniquely Indian and has a variety of meanings, holds the key to the solution. The Varnashrama method pays particular attention to the unique kind of dharma that applies to each individual. Hence, even while most people believe nonviolence to be a virtue, others—especially Kshatriyas, or military commanders sworn to defend the common people—view it as wrongdoing.

Or, to put it another way, absolute nonviolence may be suitable for a Brahmin, but not for someone whose responsibility it is to ensure that others follow the law. For someone in this position, nonviolence reverberates in more forceful tones, as protection or as a propensity to defend others. As an example, Arjuna, a Kshatriya in the Mahabharata, received the order to battle from Krishna. Millions would have died and the kingdom would have fallen into chaos if Arjuna had just sat back and preached a philosophy of nonviolence. Therefore, there are instances when violence, although under very specific conditions, becomes a stronger type of nonviolence.

In order to emphasize this argument, the Epics provide extreme examples of circumstances when only violence would suffice to achieve peaceful goals. One of the central themes of the Epics is the conflict between violence and nonviolence. One just has to consider Yudhishthira, the oldest of the Pandava Princes, as an example. He is the one who, while being a strong Kshatriya, begs for peace so often that his brothers start to think of him as a coward.

Nevertheless, he offers persuasive justifications for a life of passivity that are incontrovertible. This is confirmed by the excruciating Mahabharata war's outcome, which demonstrates that although the values of peace may be temporarily disregarded for a greater cause, such suspension always has a cost. Both parties in this conflict experienced the death of loved ones and other effects of war. Hence, even when battle is justifiable, the epics teach that it never brings about the peace and harmony that result from nonviolence, the chosen ideal.

So, it may be claimed that the Epics only support war as a last choice. Rama, on the other hand, only wanted Sita back and would have done everything to prevent a fight. That was not to be, however. The hero displays a contempt for fighting as well as the fortitude to seek out truth and justice, exactly as in the Mahabharata, when every effort was made to bring people together.

Hence, the Epics provide compassion, balanced with the need to take the appropriate action. Many attempt to address the warlike aspect of the Mahabharata and the Ramayana as well by considering them as metaphors for one another. They see Arjuna as representing Everyman, the five Pandavas as representing the five senses, and the battlefield as representing the internal conflict of Humanity.

Similarly, Rama's father's name, Dasharath, translates to "a chariot of ten," alluding to the human body, which has five functional organs and five sense organs. According to legend, he drew the three facets of nature—goodness, desire, and ignorance—embodied in his three wives, Kaushalya, Sumitra, and Kaikeyi. He also has four sons, who in actuality represent the four purposes of human existence: responsibility, economic advancement, pleasure, and liberty.

Sita symbolizes wisdom, whereas Ravana is ego and self-centeredness. The lesson is simple: all one has to do to make knowledge vanish is to embrace Ravana's weaker traits. From this vantage point, it may be argued that neither Epic had a combat.

In reality, the classic commentator Madhvacharya acknowledges that there are three different interpretations of the Epics that are all acceptable: the literal, the ethical, and the metaphorical. He makes it clear, however, that the literal interpretation is the most correct way to understand the book and that the other interpretations provide supplementary lessons from which one may learn more esoteric knowledge.

In truth, the majority of Hindus see their sacred texts as historical accounts of a period when extraterrestrial life once roamed the world and God himself came to earth to beckon his offspring to return to him.

Indeed, the most valuable lessons can only be applied if one reads the book literally. For instance, if the anguish experienced by the Pandavas and Kauravas, the disgrace Draupadi endured, the heartbreaking abduction of Sita, the harsh murder of Jatayu, and the numerous other tragedies described in the Epics, all lose their significance. When taken seriously, such human suffering makes readers' hearts swell.

The writings aim to emphasize the harsh realities of a material existence by portraying the struggles of life in a very realistic manner. They also demonstrate the virtue of courage and fortitude, whether it is demonstrated by a queen or a vulture, and that worthy aims are still valuable even if they require extreme penance and austerity to achieve.

The Epics teach us that suffering, whether it be our own or that of others, may sometimes turn out to be for the best. It may shift the focus of the intellect to spirituality and cultivate pity in the heart; it can fortify the will and encourage the growth of perseverance and patience.

These characteristics, as shown by the heroes of the Epics, are crucial for anybody attempting to cultivate a love for God. And ordinary souls may bring them into their own lives by seeing how they appear in the lives of the main characters in the Epics.

Readers are asked to internalize the traits necessary for realizing God in this manner. The primary messages of the Epics are Truth and Righteousness, both in big letters.

Both texts exhort their readers to follow Yudhishthira's example, who wanted peace and would never lie, and to avoid

Duryodhana's, who wanted only power, no matter the cost—not with overt advice but with compelling story. They also urge readers to avoid Ravana's selfishness and to follow Hanuman, who served Rama.

The Epics demonstrate how to distinguish reality from illusion and right from wrong, especially when it comes to human conduct. One of the main accomplishments of the Epics is how clearly, they describe the psychology of interpersonal interactions, demonstrating how to communicate with others in ways that eventually result in the realization of God.

A careful examination indicates that a key element of strong interpersonal interactions is the identification or creation of common ground between individuals.

The brotherly bond between the Pandava brothers, for instance, exemplifies this and encourages us to forge similar bonds in our own lives. Nevertheless, relationship education doesn't stop there. Essential abilities are required for every relationship type, and more complex partnerships cannot exist without these talents. The Epics demonstrate this via their morally upright protagonists. They also show a hierarchy, from basic obedience to friendship, from parental duty to romantic love, and from one's bond with one's nation to their relationship with God.

Each connection type needs knowledge of the relationships that came before it (in this hierarchy). In the end, a person who loves God also loves everyone. These teachings were particularly written by Vyasa for the commoners, not for the elite Brahmins who study the Vedas or spend endless hours doing rituals. It is claimed that the same Vedic knowledge is delivered here in the form of a narrative so that everyone may understand it or benefit from it.

Hence, the Epics provide practical knowledge and keen insights into human nature and interpersonal interactions that eventually help us grow in our love for God. Of course, the

THE HINDU EPICS – AN INTRODUCTION TO ANCIENT INDIA'S DEFINING MASTERPIECES.

Epics are intricate and full of subtle philosophical distinctions. Hence, it is difficult to decipher their hidden meaning or comprehend how all of their many tales and teachings relate to one another without help. It is required of one who comes from the Upanishadic tradition to study these writings at the foot of a master.

In fact, according to the Epics, without the help of a spiritual guide, the whole Hindu tradition is lost, at least in terms of its intended meaning. Although while the underlying meaning and ultimate message of the scriptures are likely to remain a mystery, one may nevertheless gain a great deal by a straightforward study of them. The quest for a genuine guru is thus strongly advised throughout these works.

The Epic has a pragmatic idealist viewpoint and a profound understanding of human frailty, greed, and aggression. The holy books advise aiming for better comprehension while enlisting the aid of spiritual experts.

THE HINDU EPICS – AN INTRODUCTION TO ANCIENT INDIA'S DEFINING MASTERPIECES.

The epic hero's world is not unlike from our own. Life pulls individuals toward renunciation and a religious way of life, and finally, of course, they succumb to death. It is a world in which people work, raise children, and deal with an all too often corrupt society. Epic heroes strive hard to uphold moral principles and do their best to make the world a better place to live.

It's true that their world is full with extraordinary creatures and abilities that are unfathomable to most people. Nonetheless, they are quite similar to us in terms of our aspirations, needs, and objectives; as a result, their lives might serve as models for our own. We should first notice that they all acknowledge spiritual preceptors.

Beyond any one particular lesson, such as the value of embracing a spiritual teacher, the Epics aim to provide their readers with a bridge between their world and ours. And the main way they do this is through interacting with others. The Ramayana in particular demonstrates how to deal with people in every setting and in any form of relationship. It starts with Rama's character, who personifies dharma and is the epitome of responsibility, honesty, and harmony. He is a devoted husband, the perfect son, and the perfect king.

Sita is the ideal wife—beautiful, virginal, and devoted, but also independent and bright. For their older brother Rama, for whom they would do everything, Lakshman and his siblings are devoted helpers and buddies. Hanuman is the perfect servant, blindly following his master's orders and attending to his wants with unwavering affection.

Ravana and the terrible creatures who surround him, on the other hand, serve as examples of the perils of giving in to desire and ego. Before making a commitment, we are instructed to think it through carefully.

King Dasharath's suffering, which was a consequence of his pledge to Kaikeyi, serves as an example of this. Yet, his story also demonstrates the value of honoring your word, no matter how painful the outcome.

Rama, who decides to leave for the wilderness and give up an entire kingdom merely to follow his father's vow, is the only person with integrity comparable to his.

The Epic also emphasizes the value of living in harmony wherever we may be and being appreciative of our possessions, no matter how little they may be, via the lives of Sita and Rama in their forest hermitage. They might have continued to live there indefinitely, but a terrible villain destroyed their exclusive paradise. Yet even then, they were ready to make amends.

The struggle between Rama and Ravana, or between the Pandavas and the Kauravas, ultimately revolves on the forces attempting to disturb cosmic order. This disturbance affects human society, the realm of the gods, and nature itself on three different levels. For instance, Ravana undermined the authority of the gods by developing superhuman abilities via yogic practices and weaving talents, exploiting those abilities for selfish means. In a similar way, he took control of other selfish individuals, and the two of them together formed an army that terrorized and exploited humanity. Eventually, he defiled nature via sensual behavior and abuse of his surroundings. The book also demonstrates his hostility against nature through his conflicts with Hanuman and Jatayu. And if Duryodhana's life is examined, a comparable event takes place.

The Epics therefore teach that until we understand the value of liberation, of freedom from discord and disruption—from aversion to dharma—we are doomed to suffer or enjoy life in a world of duality, a world that is subpar to the spiritual realms of existence promised by both the Ramayana and the Mahabharata.

The process of learning to completely appreciate nature, to appropriately engage with others, and, ultimately, to attain transcendence, must be reversed if we are to reach these later realms.

THE HINDU EPICS – AN INTRODUCTION TO ANCIENT INDIA'S DEFINING MASTERPIECES.

The Epics guide us through each world in a logical way. We must get familiar with the manners of the material world until we are free from worldly worries.

Understanding the Vedas, practicing charity, compassion, and nonviolence, along with having respect for both environment and our fellow people, all enable life to thrive in this world and are essential building blocks on the path to a life of spiritual achievement.

Yet finally we must transcend the dichotomies of worldly life, such as joy and sorrow, success and failure, and gain and loss, which, according to the Epics, are only different manifestations of the same reality. And we must take risks while starting along the spiritual road.

According to Krishna, the emergence and eventual departure of pleasure and misery are akin to the onset and conclusion of the winter and summer seasons, as stated in the Bhagavad-Gita (2.14). We must learn to bear them without being irritated since they can only be caused by sensory perception; otherwise, we are all different shades of Duryodhana and Ravana.

Yet with dharma and a focus on spiritual advancement, we may cross the chasm between heaven and earth and approach the Lord with the same ardor as Arjuna and Hanuman did.

ABOUT THE AUTHOR

Kiran Atma was born a Hindu and has been a practicing Pagan and Witch since hitting puberty. Kiran continues to study and analyze the history and contemporary practices associated with his faith and craft as seen worldwide while sharing the same with the wider community.

Printed in Great Britain
by Amazon